Commonwealth of Wing

Also by Pamela Alexander

Navigable Waterways

.

Pamela Alexander

Commonwealth
of Wings

An Ornithological

Biography

Based on the Life of

John James Audubon

To Richard Marius —
with very best wishes

Pamela Alexander

Wesleyan University Press

Published by University Press of New England

Hanover and London

WESLEYAN UNIVERSITY PRESS
Published by University Press of New England, Hanover, New Hampshire 03755

Printed in the United States of America   5   4   3   2   1
CIP data appear at the end of the book

I would like to thank the Bunting Institute of Radcliffe College for a fellowship, during which I began this project. I am also grateful to those who provided helpful comments on the manuscript, along with encouragement: Wendy Battin, John G. Case, Martha Collins, Laura Fargas, Jorie Graham, Linda Gregerson, Jay Klokker and Gary J. Quigley. This book is for my mother and father.

"Sight" appeared in *Field* as "Audubon Remembers American Falls"; "At Coueron. My First Gun," "Inventory. Journal," and "Aboard the *Ripley*" in *Margin* as "Audubon at 13, as Revolution Begins in France," "Audubon Takes Inventory," and "Audubon aboard the *Ripley*"; "Letter to Victor," "Losses" (2), and "Reprise" (1) in *Michigan Quarterly Review*; "Arrangements," "My Ornithology Proceeds," "I Imagine Thee," and "Return" appeared in *Shankpainter 30*.

Imagine a landscape wholly American, trees, flowers, grass, even the tints of the sky and the waters, quickened with a life that is real, peculiar, trans-Atlantic. It is a real and palpable vision of the New World, with its atmosphere, its imposing vegetation, and its tribes that know not the yoke of man. On twigs, branches, bits of shore, copied by the brush with the strictest fidelity, sport the feathered races, in the size of life, each in its particular attitude, its individuality and peculiarities. The sun shines athwart the clearing in the woods; the swan floats suspended between a cloudless sky and a glittering wave; strange and majestic figures keep pace with the sun.

—Philarete-Chasles, of Audubon's work, 1826

Contents

Commonwealth of Wings

I. 1785–1803

Audubon Enfant

I First
met the light and shook it
Aux Cayes, my mother la créole Rabin
who dies. I am one. Father finds
for me a stepmother and they
together a half-
sister, Muguet called Rosa,
& he is away. In his fields
I cut pieces of cane for me & Rosa
to suck. I am Jean.
My father *marin* learned
this language in an English prison.
Later I count my days from France sometimes,
this place Saint Domingue *maman* hard
to remember. New

world it is, my warm
island, wilderness churning
beyond the lines of coffee plants. The woman
names me again *Fougère* you would say Fern,
names are charms and we need them.
There are places I cannot take the little one.
Edges of things are dangerous—where
sea and land meet, or field and forest,
things get loose from their names.
On the edge of my family I call myself
LaForêt my first self before I knew
French or african or english words.
I saw red birds sign themselves in air
before they sang, flourishing.
"Parroquet. Trogon." She carried me outdoors
& I reached for them, my stepmother said.
I am Jean Jacques Fougère LaForêt Rabin
Audubon.

We Lose St. Domingue

My island has been gone for days, it shrank & flattened
& then sank like a skimmed stone. Rosa
chuckled along with the water & didn't notice.
Father calls them rooster tails, the white arcs
our ship trails at her fastest, when he is happy
& says the waves are French
because they wear berets. We lean
into the wind, we lean to France because
the island darkened, the servants
muttered among themselves & wouldn't answer.
Now I have no place to go. The waves march past us
in rows, & talk, & make a chorus
behind my father's stories, who never said so much
ashore. Birds balance on the wind beside our sails
or make chevrons on the big shoulders of clouds
so they are captains. He says
France will show me new animals & birds
and I will have as many islands as I want,
I'll jingle them like pocket change, he says I am
his little archipelago,
& I think how far we are going,
how big the world will be when we stop.

Nantes, the Revolution

Nantes. Geography, music
threaten daily, *école*.
Four different seasons,
& rabbits & Larks are shy,
no sugar birds here to pick
insects from furniture, neatly.
Buildings dress in uniform,
steep slate roofs the same blues
& grays as pigeons that settle
& scatter hourly from spires
where metal flowers swing
& bang. Windows close to keep outside

out, where I find
muskrats, watch their whiskers move
& the color of their fur
change as it dries. Meetings,
loud talk, then not school but
siège, the city slams shut, bells are unmounted
& melted for cannon, the mouths of waterspouts
taken from squares, coffins raised & opened
for their lead. That is bad, will bring
the dead among us & no one here knows the words
to sing or where to pick the cleansing herbs.
Guns mark the hours now, raggedly,
some so close that when they speak my body rings
& I am disconnected, float
without hearing my boots hit
the stone street where I am fastest among grandfathers
& bell-shaped women. My paper boat rides
to the current, I race along the bank

& find him & fight still
as I do for animals but

there is nothing to scare, only
man-shape in wet clothes, in reeds, it doesn't matter
his mouth is full of mud.
Old men bury him & he is not
the last I find
this spring.

The Siege Outlasted,

life is worse. Shivering royalists stand
at the cathedral wall, those who faint
are shot first
so not to be overlooked.
Townspeople watch but only the muskets clap.
Flies come long before the carts. Loads
are thrown into the Loire until the current slows
then dropped midstream
but the bodies make another bridge below,
& swell, & won't budge. We have
no other place. Fevers take
as many, more, than bullets, & death seems less
because there are many.

At Coueron. My First Gun.

Mama & I
& Rosa, we hope never to meet
another war. Here
the land is flat & trim, sheep
swerve together, hedges & fences
keep order. I explore
margins & flawed places
while Rosa's piano turns
a pretty flurry. I take chocolate
in waxy papers & a basket
to bring back nests & lichens, more strange
than my lessons. The daily murders of the city are far, fewer,
then stop, & I forget them.

We grow
apart, my sister
and I, she domestic, says
my blown eggs & stuffed birds
stink. I close the door.

I shoot well, corks I toss
come down in showers, my fingers gleam
with powder. The gun kicks my shoulder,
its shout & smell clear me.
The bird falls,
always. I watch its color & shine & flare
for weeks before I fire, but my sketch preserves
only its deadness. I burn
my pencil's generation of cripples
on my birthday.

Sometimes I sleep
near my Originals, on leaf litter

beneath the trees they close their eyes in,
sometimes I lie awake in the quiet house
& listen to the nightwatch
kept by the river, old water clock,
& by whickering horses standing
to their sleep.

Father's Home,

leg-wounded, lung-sore, *lieutenant de vasseau*
pensioned. Puts the box of medals in the bottom of his trunk,
sits in the courtyard by the orangery
and dozes when the sun is on him. White petals
fall & mingle with his hair.
The chair tilts on the flags, he starts awake
and finishes reading. Each letter
makes the news bad & worse, finally
the plantation in St. Domingue is lost
complete. La Gerbetière, this place
of limestone walks & box-maze, parterre & pigeon lofts,
has two journals of land. With a farm called Mill Grove
in Pennsylvania, America, it is his last fortune.

His mind is busy with wars. The world
is always burning somewhere, he says:
he smells it. He has a sip of wine
& coughs again, and says he fears
my conscription. I will hide, pockets full
of shot & powder, chalk, paper, cheese—
he shakes his head too slowly to mean No.

We Are Gentlemen Abroad

My French partner's passport's
Dutch, I'm native to New Orleans
to escape Napoleon's levies,
to which

our ship struck by privateers & stripped
of wine, pigs, our best two sailors,
& kept in *Rattlesnake*'s lee
a day, in pistol range,
off Sandy Hook New York

is trifling.

Landed,
sunburned & excited,
I learn that the body remembers
motion: rooms & streets swoop
seawise. I laugh at my sailor's walk
but am suddenly weak—

burning, I ride
long arcs, moan, crest
in sunlight & slide, dizzy, down. Is it water
makes such huge noise? Some
dark thing looms, I struggle,
drenched, in a disarray of quilts—

So my English comes pirated,
fevered, Quakered. They wear
gray dresses, & when they open windows
trees waver in ordinary light
& I am John James, agent

in America for Audubon *père*
who is words on paper here,
an Atlantic of days away
from Rozier & me, men of business.

II. 1803–1808

Mill Grove

My life is curious, immense, unruled
as its new country in which my father's wars
mutter only in the occasional basso
among the river's many voices. High in one rocky bank
I find a large dry cave and draw there;
a phoebe finds it too, then another.
Their conversations transpire
above the pink bells of anemones, above trilliums
white & red. I follow the creek
called Perkiomen. I follow deer trails
& bear tracks & birdsong,
I follow currents of air. Soon every tree
knows my name, the cane brake rattles
to attention! I draw from life now
& finish nothing, dissatisfied, make outlines
of hundreds of flying swifts and finches,
lively but incomplete, & fill my book
with the cooperative faces of my neighbors
the Bakewells. He, William, though english,
is a good shot and possessed
of handsome daughters, excellent
pointer dogs, and a son Thomas. Around us the woods cool
& flare with foxes, the Schuylkill River
hardens for our skating parties
& we are rampant.

The Englishman's Eldest Daughter

We watched, Lucy Bakewell and I,
through the open window
in the drawing room at Fatland Ford,
her father's pillared home I call the Parthenon
to her. Within inches of the sill
the nesting Wren takes ants and spiders,
still struggling, from her mate's bill.
When he flies into the room
& sings, I slide the sash down gently
and he lets Lucy
touch him; Lucy holds him in her hand.

Balancing

I have always slept the way I ride, dance, and shoot—
when I want, and well. Tonight
sleep is harder than waking,
my muscles at ready as if for danger, here
at midnight on the edge of an obscure continent
with my house and farm holding me,
quiet. My heart startles me, its surging so close
to the surface. Is it always so? To put
the parts of sleep together I tell
my muscles one by one to be loose. Why should I not
sleep? I was sick once, my fever on landing,
but I have never been afraid.
My heart slows. Under my hand it kicks

evenly, like a boy sitting on a wooden bridge
who swings his lower legs as if walking
on the green current below
while he thinks he is not afraid, thinks
he doesn't mind that his friends have slid out of sight
leaving him perched, alone, *too high!* although
he saw the water accept and then
hold the others up, saw their backs gleam
in the dark river, their heels
graze the surface from beneath in a slow flutter,
although he knows from lesser jumps
that the rush of water past his ears will sound
like applause—

falling, I wake.

The Current

Lucy, look at that root
diverting the current, leaving a still place
where water & bank fit together
perfectly, the water rising slightly
around each stone to hold it, intimate
as a nest around a dove. See
the green rays that the sun behind us draws
on the water, rays streaming outward
from the shadows of our heads
as if we were painted saints, see
when we move closer we perceive
each other's radiance more clearly? Closer.

Letter to Lucy

Pennsylvanian earth resembles us—
red flesh veiny with water, perfused
with motion & stirred by all the quirky Energies
of life, ours
or a windy marsh with bitterns and ducks—that's
a business fit for a man like myself, strong & quick
as you can find, Lucy, and not to be found much longer
in the pestilent port of New York
as apprentice-clerk in a commercial house.
I did not realize how dearly I would detest it,
seventy-five thousand persons calling one place
home! & me a merchant! My life has not subdued itself
to Indigo & wine. Thoughts of thee
were like the silver thread I tied last spring
around the phoebe's leg, knotted loose
to cause no injury but to hold
forever. & soon I will return from a year
of scribbling bad english in a dim room
to show your father my worth. My sum would be
no greater for any more of that. One year given him,
Love, I offer you the rest.

Our Conspiracy of Pleasure

I came from wildness and across it, at large
among waves the size of this house, my journeys since that crossing
shorter but innumerable. I have pressed my bootsoles
into mud & moss & dry leaf duff, improvising paths
in rangy curvilinear abundance
as I followed my whim
& joy, that flew ahead, half-seen.
Your mother's frown, your father's sombre approval
blow away in the vastness where waves
lean & fall & resume, where new leaves loosen.
My hopes for us change as fast
as light on water. I am rich! You are!
Your brothers & sisters dance, the candles gutter
to their motion. Tomorrow, Lucy, Wife, we'll start
our wedding trip, sunlit, we'll wade through the shallow mist
that rises from April snow, then slide slowly
a thousand miles south,
clothes and drawings bundled,
flatboated, Ohio-floated,
Kentucky bound,
with stores of things to sell
because we must. But we will not
complicate ourselves. Let others keep the books!

III. 1808–1826

We Find the Outset Erratic

The first day the wind comes against us
so hard a man can't turn toward it & breathe,
and we tie up in the lee of a bend
since the bulky craft makes no way. Among a dozen
of us passengers only Rozier is impatient, counting the hours
as money lost. I lie with thee beneath four blankets
in the half-open cabin, pleased,
listening to twigs skitter across the canvas roof.
The wind subsides at dusk, & the river changes
its shaggy coat for close-lapped triangles
that shiver apart & reappear. Among the men
I am clairvoyant of weather, the captain's
confrère, and best
at pushing us free of mud bars.

The current is our pilot now
that moves us faster in the narrow channels
beside shrubbed islands like large animals
grazing on bottom weeds. Salt pork & biscuit
is our fare, though I volunteer to shoot a fat fresh dinner
given half an hour ashore. The captain
refuses. Let him unstick us then
at the next impasse. Are we alone
in leisureliness? Yes, & doomed I see
to an efficient honeymoon! Still
Rozier fumes. In Louisville
we'll set up shop and make him rich—he has nothing
better to do—while thou & I will study to be
Savants of happiness.

The Inn, Louisville

I feel you rend.
When I hear his cry
I think my life has flown
to another body.
And so it has.
Victor Gifford Audubon
slides into this world
on the third floor of the Indian Queen
at leaf-height, at daybreak
in my twenty-fourth year.

A Visit from Wilson

Business is a burden. We need cash.
The resolution of two unpleasantnesses
charms me with simplicity—sell the business! At last
life allows Gain and Ease to agree. Who would buy
trouble? My partner Rozier is our profit here,
who will be paid in kind for being mercenary
& Dull witted, as he showed himself again
when that odd Scotsman visited the store.
Naturalist, he called himself, & carried dozens
of drawings, Folio size. Spread on the counter
they astonished me. His best
were small-headed Flycatcher & Mississippi Kite, neither
as life-like as I have them. He talked of publication
& I was curious about his life altogether—
but Rozier, muttering the while in French
which the Scot seemed not to know,
burst out in english worse than mine
that I would have no more money to throw away
especially for silly pictures. Today the stranger
is gone, & the querulous flute from his room
late at night. Rozier sulks. The man's a mule.
I'll put this business on his back.

At Ease

If I had known such contentment existed
I would have sought it sooner. I knew
I wanted thee, & now
the home I didn't know I longed for
is real, built at Bayou Sara of logs & lichens & of our selves.
My life is with you & with my wandering,
the mill runs itself which suits me better than a store.
Geese preen in the dooryard & spread their clipped wings.
Soon Victor will be hunting bigger game
than the dozen turtles he has grabbed, giggling.
Now he watches them sun, delicious,
inconspicuous, in the fenced pond.
Johnny, who came while I was away,
is old enough just to rock & be sung to,
Sur le pont d'Avignon l'on y danse l'on y danse.
Our few disturbances are natural: storms,
& ice on the river breaking in spring
with a sound like artillery.

Disaster

I have cause to despair and will not.
I owed & was owed, availed myself of a dozen niggling Partners,
my steam Mill did worse and I was forced to sell my horses,
house, land, the unfortunate Machine itself, now stilled
except squirrel-flickered & shouted at by Jays
that eat from open sacks of grain.
Jailed for debt, I do not repent the three good years
wooden shafts turned at the center of my excursions.

The air is odd, now, empty of racket
that attended all my homecomings, grown noisier otherwise
with the children, one old enough to follow me.
He must see how few men bow to his father on the street
although I decline to notice, just as I ignored the garment
the gaoler tossed me after taking my silk shirt
to sell with all else incidental. Long hair
fell over my bare shoulders & warmed me
until Lucy brought another shirt,
less fine but my own. The sheriff said I acted like an Indian
which I will take to mean honorably & misunderstood.
I own now these clothes, one gun, drawings considered worthless
& my confidence. The drawings must be seen. I will be admired
by more than myself & family, or I mistake my efforts.

A Profitable Life

eludes me. Risen again to the world, I thought
to settle, taxidermist at the Museum in Philadelphia,
but have stuffed myself most industriously
out of business, even did fishes after all the Fowl.
The man who hired me has left and no one else
knows how to sign my name to a note? Lucy
no matter. We have been unmoneyed before.
My purpose, that had staggered,

lifts. It makes me simple, a curve
my hand draws without government by a round thought.
Enjoying my life I will enlarge it
& for this must peregrinate, reckless in others' eyes
but regular to my Plan
& you will be my astronomer, you will see its shape, my hope
realized, ah! thrush by thrush.

Portraits

I give my self a year to make one Hundred
drawings & here begin with my young friend
Joseph Mason, & Dash the game-wise dog,
our first productions a Telltale Godwit and hermit Thrush
& further a portrait of a shoemaker and his Wife
in fair trade for two pairs of boots, Dash needing none.
We take our work & comforts from the woods
as far as New Orleans, a penny between us.

We will stay the winter. I wear my good shirt
to the bookseller's to glimpse Wilson's book
which is dear. Joseph & I finish 20 drawings
including boat tailed Grackle, brown pelican
and a Warbler not described by the Scot. I am improved,
laying a ground of water colours under the pastels
to prevent appearance of the paper, but the work slows
with necessity, the city parries employment with expense.
A few warm days we set up on the street & draw from memory
faces of persons famous here, to show our skill
& have some reward. Twice we are awakened
to take likenesses of old men dying, and one clergyman
disinters his young daughter that we can preserve her Forever.
In March having made portraits everywhere
we find no more sitters & leave, pockets full of chalk.

Arrangements

The world changes in a wing beat.
Aboard a steamer, travel for me & companions
traded for three days work on a Steam Co. sign,
I meet an agreeable lady Mrs Pirrie
who much admires me as others have
and offers a position as others have not.
We talk of my project, the book I want to make
& our talk grows warmer & the air takes on
a fragrance of magnolias as we move upriver
and she, intelligent Benefactor, confirms
my belief that Fortune breathes
in each of us, if we persist: not luck
but an answer to our working joy. I am Tutor
in drawing, music & dancing, with time
to hunt & draw, & paid,
& board for Mason too. Warblers sing intermittently
among mottled beech & yellow Poplar
as we approach the settlement.

My Ornithology Proceeds

For five months the magnolias
have steadied us, five months of sturdy work.
Joseph is able, drafting plants and other
Accessories. Only my student
lags, her sketches sullen, her health poxy, and I
have been declared a cause! or drawing has,
by her young and jealous Physic, who thinks me
a fearless blade. & so I am, but innocent of desire
for plaintive, moist Miss Pirrie. He has prescribed
four months' abstinence from lessons
but she may eat whatever stirs her fancy. She calls
for sugar cakes all afternoon, and I am relieved
of educating her artful urges. I take
my freedom quickly to the forest.

Letter to Lucy

Mlle Pirrie is betrothed making Tutors
superfluous. Joseph & I, banished by love & resentment
from the rivery murmurous sanctuary,
return to New Orleans, purse & portfolio fattened, jubilant,
my voyage nearly possible. We are remembered
& recommended by those we have drawn
but new faces wanting description are few.
We inquire next of businesses despite experience
that they have little need for artists. So it is again.
We persist, to become Masters of tavern murals & smithy signs,
& once a month I sweat in my best clothes
instructing a dozen young souls to sarabande. Joseph
cannot help in this, nor tell gallop from gavotte.
We live with care
& save my passage.

Three months I have been a stranger to my journal
but regular & faithful at length
in letters to thee, who reply
thou art jealous of a thousand inhabitants of Air.
As am I, & grateful for thy accord.
I cannot live with thee until I make a better husband,
bolster my regard now bankrupt among friends
& everywhere. I will transform.

Losses

Joseph left today, we had great pain
at parting. His father has died, & besides
I can show him nothing more of draughtsmanship.
I gave him chalks
to work his way with, and the double barrel gun
I bought in Philadelphia. He turned only once
& did not raise his hand.

It is spring again & our lives precarious.
Here is the city, its squabbly shapes
cocked about, then the marshes & mists & mud,
then the great pelagic openness—
the mind can't support the whole at once. I cut
a blooming stick of wisteria & return to our room.

Journal, at Sea

Outwardly this book appears a ledger
& will indeed be my Account. Now I leave my woodsman life
to broker a prospectus: all the Birds of America,
in the size of nature, described by me.
Philadelphian friends are sure no one here
will publish me against Wilson, & I sail to Europe
to find support from lords and learned Societies,
& superior engraving. Behind me a steamboat churns upriver
with two boxes of flowering plants for Lucy.

Off Cuba, intense heat. My hopes
are in the breeze, which is often contrary.
Evolutions of large Phalaropes distract me: they fly low,
legs hanging & feet patting the sea with extended webs. I draw
a rudder fish, an exhausted Rice bunting on a spar,
& I sleep generously.

I catch a Dolphin, observe closely its twenty tints
that fade to a common gray in seconds, as its convulsions
proceed to twitches & then stillness
on the hot deck. An auburn whale breaches
& springs its valved breath so close we are misted.
But I have no feeling, as if watching myself from the masthead.
As a child I sailed this ocean wave by wave.
Now thoughts for my future fly across my mind
with every eastward wing that passes
this cotton-stuffed ship wallowing under slumped sail.

After a week the light, wrong-headed breezes give way.
Our motion stiffens and we pass Cuba. I am restless with hope
& ignorance. Friends, Wife, America, farewell!

IV. 1826–1829

Spirits

Uneasy, arrived, distributing politeness & met coldly.
Is this *à l'anglais*? I smile. At the custom house
outraged, smiling, charged two pence
each portfolio, already paid. Now it is Sunday, and dull
at every window. Thy long skirt rustles like a curtain. Thou sayst
Dear friend how can you think it dull? I am beyond
your improvement. Dull! There is no one I may talk to freely. I talk
to myself, but not freely, here, having secrets,
that I am poor, that my birth—no, I will not discuss my original
poverty, or good fortune as my father called it. He must have meant
his own pleasure. Here I am, poised to meet Society, legitimate men all.
Should a naturalist not be natural? The fact lies dumbly
beneath a stone on St. Domingue, itself
a stone basking in the sun below America. Gone. I speak
of my mother. —I have frequently believed myself
a fool, the opinion variously received. This evening
I think so again, more deeply than ever. I am sure
I saw the wife of Geo. Keats today. *How can that be?*
If I did not see the wife of Geo. Keats of London &tc. &tc.
(I will write no more etceteras, they dull my pen)
then undoubtedly I saw her spirit—oh, do not dim,
thou advisor, Navigator, leader of my motions, mental
or physical, vertical or horizontal, &tc (damn the &tcs)!
Sterne, yes Sterne I believe, said horizontals
are the most congenial patterns for all feelings whatsoever.
This last thought is strenuous, my dear, is it not? To thee I raise
my Sunday cup. God bless the merry Sterne,
God Bless! Bless Geo. Keats! His wife! Mine!
And bless the wild grape— Wait!
                                        Gone.
Having seen thee for a moment
I will let thee go, back to Beech Woods,
my love. And as you have not touched
your glass of port, I'll do so. To your health!

Letter to Lucy

My birds exhibit themselves, as I do. Approved, both.
I am passed hand to hand, my dress & locks remarked
(the latter for their length & bear grease brightness),
my owl hoot & turkey call requested by professors,
consuls, doctors, bon vivants & Ladies, my stories
of American trees smiled at, none grows here
beyond a sapling. Signs warn of *trespass*,
the land is owned entirely, paths walled
above my height, as if to look were sin.
No one here has seen a moccasin, a garfish sunning,
the pink ibis & her spatulate companion
—lonely. Three ships arrive this week
without the letters I know thou hast sent by now.
I scarcely sleep, rinse my mind with an early walk
& blackbirds in an uproar. At six I am sleeves up
at work in oil on a Trapped Otter, at eight my every line
observed by a growing crowd of critics
behind my elbows. My style puzzles. I do not
always think of thee Lucy
but thy presence moves in my mind like a shy bird
that flies before me, bush to bush.

From My Journal

Liverpool's market invites me
with fishes and fruits, enormous cheeses, crates
of hens eggs layered in oatstraw, the myriad commodities displayed
within a building arranged in spacious avenues,
the whole so lighted with gas
that at ten o'clock I tell the colors
of the irises of caged pigeons. The city without is lit, too.
After three weeks I do not look on everything
as a stranger, but I am not at home. The confidence
I have been at times accused of—thou knowst well—
is primitive, and fits me for befriending forests
more than lords. But lords I do, and gratefully. My business
does increase, introductions beget introductions. I count first
among new friends the Rathbones, a family of such kindness
I find hope that my awkwardness will abate. I long
to summon thee for them
as I do for myself. —I had much trouble
untying the fastener of my portfolio last night,
after a walk in their garden, after dinner.
I knew again from the talk all evening
they are of good judgment. The lights arranged, the company
quiet, I turned my pages & heard the tissues whisper, one by one.
All praised! I pleased! Oh, what can I hope?

Etude

Finally my Otter stands. After looking at it some minutes
I walk to the Mersey, the day so still I hear the paddles
of a steamboat on the river Dee, eight miles distant,
its course flagged skyward by smoke.
I hire a car and take the otter
to my friend old Mrs Rathbone, to ease my going.
She asks me to write often. She has a robin
I have been careful not to shoot these months,
& as I say Good-bye it flies about the room.
My life is a superimposition of partings. I take
a public carriage to Manchester, past fields
abounding with Hares & partridges
raised tame & killed without pursuit.

Interlude

A grainy Fog dampens my senses & slows the wheels
of the borrowed trap. No landscape passes
to demonstrate my progress, even the front half of the horse
uncertain. The road starts up, stony or bare, only
just beneath his hooves. This is the way
to Matlock, hamlet of thy birth Lucy
now much reduced in numbers. I stop
in the lane. The great mist, which granted
a single roadside fern, a single speckled rock,
now lifts its skirts around the stone church. The notion
overcomes me that it is like my Project,
clear and sensible at its base and aspiring
to delicate extensions, obscure
in the dense atmosphere. I walk
about the church completely, as if to find
someone; I believe I go about, although
I feel neither gay nor sad, vigorous nor fatigued,
unsure that I breathe or walk, as if this day
is apart from my life and I shall have no memory of it tomorrow.

Edinburgh

This morning I opened a window onto yet a third city
and leaned out, hands on the sill, to look for persons
coming to see my work describing Birds those exponents
of magnificence, of wilderness unimaginable
in this smoky place—creatures who bind the sky
to the earth these sensible people walk upon, the earth
that feels them walking!—Well. I stood there
staring out, so long

that ladies & errand boys who passed below
must have marked me mad—then I slapped the sill
and bolted down the stairs straight to Mr Neill's counting house
at Fish Market Close, along the row of clerks
whose faces turned up as I passed, their paleness like foam sliding
along a wave top. I told their employer I was a simple person
of direct manner and did not wish to offend,
but as he had not responded to my letter of introduction since two days
I begged him to tell me if I was not good enough to be considered
and I would be on my way. I would have said more
but he took both his hat and my arm
and propelled me to the business of Mr Lizars, Engraver,
who took my other arm, and so to my lodging.
My anxiety was great, overcoming my embarrassment
upon noticing I had worn slippers the whole event. (This business
of civilization is fiddly—one must not walk out without hat and key
and purse, I disprefer it.) Mr Lizars talked all the way of Selby,
had I seen his drawings? They were superb! None better! I must! Etc!
I showed Cock Turkey, Hawk pouncing on partridges, Mocking bird
with Rattlesnake. His chatter stopped
as though some agitated parrot, shot,
dropped from its branch. He said "My god I have never seen
the like." At Great Footed Hawks his arms fell to his side.
"I will publish these." Dear friend we have done it.

Letter to Victor

Your Father who drew & followed Nature
has vanished, his place supplied to one of similar countenance
whom all mistake and celebrate, who does no work but consumes honors
at dinners, at parties & soirées, at lectures of botany, discussions
of philosophy, advertisements, pronouncements, assurances & advisements!
for whom forests and their inhabitants are transformed
to stories for skeptical faces. He lives in London, this Shard
of a former life, and today is begged to be the artful guest
—at Breakfast! who will soon vaporise
into a Flock of words & fly, leaving a suit of clothes dropped
upon the pavement for those requiring marvels.

A silence to you and yr Mother, my pen not sharpened
to letters or the daily book for three months: Lizars sent
the first plates, true & delicate even to the translucence of feathers
and then news that his colorists had struck, he will not pay them
their demand. —I sought again an Engraver
of Quality. Found Mr Havell a splendid craftsman
in whose opinion producing Birds of America will take 16 years. I say
half as many, but he is old & unable to commit
in either case. Still he helped me. He knows
every printing house at work in this City & we looked together
for an artist whose lines showed not only intelligence
but joy, and after a hundred prints
we stopped at an unsigned landscape
& admired,
& at length inquired as to its maker. The old man staggered
at the name. It was his son
who graved it! His youngest, who had abandoned College
to learn his father's trade, who disapproved.
                                        Their reconciliation
brings you powerfully before my eyes. I regret not writing

& this time away. Thank you for your letters. Study
music & draw & be in the woods, take all your time. You know
the Gun I mean, it is yrs now, God Bless.

I Imagine Thee

Sometimes fervent, sometimes arrested of hope
& absent from thee almost three years—
Yet please understand a While longer.
Have passage to America in a week, will spend a month or two
at Great Egg Harbor to redo some early pieces, especially
the blue-headed vireo, & find the winter wren's nest.
I must draw, the more now I am fortunate.

But soon I will walk the lane, will not hear
ordinary noises, the music & stir of the woods
passing around me. I will knock at the familiar door
& beg to introduce myself Mr Audubon, late of London
but truly of every where a migratory person
who greatly desires thy Company.
                              —I see a smile
I have seen in air many times, now on thy lips, and thou sayst
"I know something of this man." We kick the door shut.

Return

I came along the path at dusk
toward a figure stooped above the woodpile, I was not sure who
until she turned, arms full, & saw me
and stepped back, as if afraid—Lucy,
of me? Or that the Vision of a man was only air,
sly manufacture of desire, impossible of touch?—I was not able
to say a word. Each stared.
And then I dropped my gun & bag and picked her up,
wood & all, a thing no vision could do, nor could it kiss her
quite as well as I did, then, and all the way to the house.
As the wood was difficult I did not attempt the door
& left it standing open. On the stairs she laughed & cried
alternately, as did I, and as we gained the bedroom
there came a great clatter of falling sticks.

V. 1829–1840

After the Stir & Sweep of Travel,

inward shocks accrue. The boy Johnny I left is no boy now
& knows me not, pulls away
and toys among his pockets. I fear
you have indulged him, as I was & wish was not.
Arrangements vegetal and social have not stayed
where left, nor should I expect so,
except that they retire in a traveller's mind
to half-thought, sheltered from motions that revise the world
in such easeful increments as to be invisible
to the daily sight. My sons
strangely tall, all towns bigger
& the Night heron more wary, as his kind
has provided many campfires with crisp & delicate roasts.
Zephyr that stout & savvy hunter, gone.

—Victor wants to marry. I am startled, although
I suppose he is of the age. Has this been a secret
saved for my Return? Home has changed
more than I first perceived, but I will overtake
circumstances. Now let wine bloom in our best glasses.
Let's drink to the children, Lucy, and they to us! More!

I Am Restless despite Myself

All the stories I can summon I have said—
more will come I doubt not—
my mind is disarranged among its present joys,
some longed for, like thy company,
some unthought of, like Victor's choice of wife,
compounded that she is my friend Bachman's daughter.
I have all pleasures, a journey done
& one planned, and my family
with which to contemplate them both.
My government, convinced by Kings perhaps,
prove at last a friend to my work, I dine with Jackson
on turkey shot a mile from the white house,
meet Dnl. Webster who subscribes, & attorney general Butler,
and if the Seminole war does not prevent
will have a schooner of 12 tons & crew
for me & my assistants to visit Florida
—Ah! Have I told thee of my obituary
in the *Gazette*? All London startled by my misfortune
more startled yet to see a man so unconcerned with his death
as to merely dicker in the market
for a pair of Snipes and a melon. (My name changed
for Wilson's, a small matter these naturalists all a kind,
though I will not vouch for the other's opinion.) I am solid,
unharmed by the notice, electric fluid moves in me,
observatory nerves as vigilant—No
I will not go yet a while
Lucy, I cannot change this now,
I come and go—

Cape Florida

Crusader flies new cotton sails & our starry Flag atop them,
but four guns forward and a black hull
give her the look of privateer more than Navy cutter.
She pursues the tranquil business of charting
at a rate suitable for my explorations
& our rendezvous, although if pirate quarry offered
I would be abandoned eagerly. The interior
is dark, delirious with insects; snakes & vines swarm
through huge cypresses, while below them
shallow-watered alligator country alternates
with thick stands of palmetto, nettles,
& wild plum. Navigable streams are rare
& it is nowhere good for walking. Recovery
of shot birds from the mire is difficult.
The captain expects 3 plantations from here to Texas
and of wanderers like me & my party
no one, white nor red.
                              Those we meet have ships beneath them
—eggers from Havana on their third trip this season
for eggs so plentiful that they are not counted
but sold by the gallon. One ship took 8 tons
from Sooty Tern & Noddy on one island. At such a rate
all the Specimens will be destroyed. —Further south, a sail
closes fast and runs with us: new copper gleams
through the clear wave tops, & on deck all is oiled
& neatly stowed. Our captain speaks of them as Wreckers,
of whom I have slanderous ideas. They are respected here,
as their Salvage sometimes rescues
the most enduring victims of disaster.

Consolation

The violence in Civilized parts is worrisome. We have old
New York Papers describing riots, I advise
thy absence from that country. We are well away,
our last named place being St. Augustine
a poor sandy town profuse of oranges, some buildings
entirely in a plaster made of coarse ground shell.
The shadows of orange trees against the brilliant walls
were pleasing, though the fruit sour.
The weather is unruly, unreasonably hot
one day & cold the next. In consolation I have seen
a new Eagle I hope to kill tomorrow.
                                                    What dangers we have
are predictable, from Nature who can be used
against herself. I do not walk into water
unless it be a living bouillabaisse. Though my legs
are bruised where the fish slap in panic
their presence ensures no alligators. Plato suffers,
for when hot his habit is to plunge into the nearest water
& swim slowly, looking sleepy, for hours,
& I prevent him. I bind his paws with leather
because they are raw, cut by the shells of raccoon oysters,
common here; he has been bit in the face twice
by Ducks, one he dropped and I shot again.
We are all Abraded, Lehman & Ward & I, from shells
& sand & Insects which are hugely plentiful
& we are welts & salt-sore scratches everyone. Please send
more good Woollen socks, the marsh & mud
& tide flats we travel wear them urgently.

Excursion

We rowed up a long creek with a sugar planter
headstrong & gritty as my younger self. At Jupiter Inlet
we were taken by darkness premature
and then a wind that struck us like boards
& kept up hard, building waves
that swept us over marshy stuff here considered land
and in their troughs slammed us down on mud
with such force we stuck & were swamped by the next crest.
We alternately shoved at the slippery hull
& clung to it as a wave roared by,
& shoved again & scrambled in & bailed. And again,
ten or a dozen rounds. —Then air suddenly calm as a cave
& the waves expiring in minutes
as they must in thin water.
We felt our way about with oars
and tied up to a wet key
which is nothing but a fence of trees around water.

At dawn we see ourselves a half mile from an island
worthy of the name, though small. For heat & fun
we fire it, watch the damp reeds explode
into dozens of marsh rabbits scattering & swimming
as we count our strokes away.

Wreck

Humid air hovered over our work; my hands slipped
on the gunstock. Beneath dense nesting sites
the ground was white with droppings
which gave off effluvia each day more repellent.
I recalled heronries on the island in Fresh Pond, near Boston,
built on the ground, but here the birds preferred mangroves
at varied heights, some drooping over black water.
On my birthday I shot with pleasure
the largest heron of my life, a new species,
called to the others "A Prize! A Prize!" after which I felt
exhausted by heat. We rested, ate soaked
biscuit & water with molasses.
                                        Toward evening
we came upon a cove where scores of limp forms
stirred in the slack tide: for some seconds I was at Nantes
again; I know not what the others thought.
Beyond the second bar an angled mast
& half a hull. We took it in
and looked at each other & away.
And then we spent a careful hour checking
the heavy cotton bales—some perfect though most burst—
wading, prodding, to ensure none of the Crew
lay lost amongst the cargo.

Air

At extremes, the glass lower than I have seen,
where the continent breaks off into scrappy keys
and alligators bellow & splash. My discomforts here
have not prevailed. Daily I lose myself & live
as Creature, hear the alarm of jay
as if jay myself. Although I shoot
& shout to my fellows, when the sounds fade

my body loosens toward the air, which is a greater body,
its brilliant passages limitless
over waves, its dark paths tilting through mangrove branches.
I share it with a commonwealth of wings.
Sometimes the ground is obscured by thousands of gannets
surging upward, wings of the closest striking my face,
and I rise, momentarily, with them.

To Lucy

My vision is perfect. Steaming upriver toward another journey
I see plainly a vireo on a fence so distant
others find no bird at all. The world seems larger, Lucy,
or I inhabit more of it. I no longer match my doubts
with fraudulent certainty, I neither covet success
nor abase myself for it.—I have Plato, who trembles
at the steamer's blast & rumble
as he never does at shots or a struggling bird.
He is thin & needs rest.

I miss thee more deeply now
not because I am more lonely but because
I am astounded by happiness in a way I had Forgot,
at home in the whistling pulsing openness.
I have a place from which I go forth,
& it remains with me. Lucy, I am near.

Inventory. Journal.

American Harbor, Labrador, lat 50° 12′N long 23°E of Quebec

June 22. I have finished here
Arctic Tern, Brown Lark on a nest
Eider duck, Puffin (the peat-filled soil is everywhere
penetrated by their burrows), Ptarmigan
Razor billed Auk, male White Winged crossbill
female Grouse and five young, two Canada jays
one about 3 weeks old, Bunting, Loon (a difficult bird)
Red Necked Divers, one Ruby crowned Wren
an accidental Red Bellied Nuthatch blown in
female spruce Partridge with brood,
I wished not to destroy them
but my enthusiasm for Science required it.

Only settlers nearby, a French Canadian family:
an acre of potatoes planted in sand, one ox,
snow above their small windows by October.

Indians encamped: astonished us by offering
best French rum which we drank gratefully,
rubbing our hands. Told us they hunted variously before
but now shoot what pays although it is harder each time.
Marten, otter, Sables are so few the younger men
have seen none, nor tracks. These Montaignais are like
the southern Nations in that we take their food & hope.

July 1. A nameless cove. Steep cliffs surmount our mast
on all sides and in the dimness ravens glide, croaking.
The rocks break so that climbing is anxious
and in the country beyond we sink to our knees in mosses.
Elsewhere the surface waves at our step

and we fear to plunge through the vegetable layer.
Birches whiter than I have seen. Red streams.
Blue land snails. Gypsum.

A sealer's cabin: stove, bed, flour barrel
full of seine floats. A journal in a moldy book,
in French, two distinct hands. The whole
abandoned, all the seals caught.

July 4. We would go farther North but prevented by an iceberg
at the cove's mouth. Light green, it glitters
even in the shade of cliffs, in appearance a storm condensed.
The captain says it will melt below & turn, enormously
slow, with a sound of war. So we make our holiday here,
the ship tucked in a crevice like a Foolish Guillemot,
and roast our last mutton quarter as the light shifts
toward blue. It will brighten soon enough.
John takes off thick mittens and sends notes from his violin
to sweeten the throats of ravens settled amongst the highest rocks.

Aboard the Ripley

Not old. But feel sinews working
where once was thoughtless agency.
I am glad of my body its endurance to the completion
of this work, soon. Colors still good despite the salt.
A ship however is a careless place to draw. Most troublesome
is the dripping while I work, not only rain
but fog collecting & falling from spars
to my table, beneath the hatch for light. I cover
all but the wing or foot that is the focus of my brush
until this puts a strangeness on me
lest a part offend the whole. In this desolate howling place
I feel my sight enlarge, my work smaller against these rocks
than in the sitting rooms of Scotland.
My science, drawing, my life, my sons & theirs
all part of a thing I never conceived when the instinct
came to me to shape a bird on paper. I mean
the conversation along the centuries
between wildness & the need to tame. —Weary,
coming to this book, light begins at two of the morning
and I rise & draw. Robins sing nearly at midnight.
The weather afflicts, even in harbor the motion high enough
to sicken us some days. Twice the anchor drags
despite chain with links the size of my knees.

Inventory. Resolve.

This week I have as many years
as a year has weeks
or a deck, cards

and 1837 comes up a joker, banks
& businesses fail & blame van Buren,
my Birds falter, Subscribers tire
at ten years, a guinea a number.
Lucy I tire too. I think no longer this Work
will be the end of work, my efforts
sound as ever but profit taken
by the Panic. Texas was huge & dirty
& poor, I walked to the President's mansion
in water to my ankles, a log house
of two rooms. Mr Houston is taller even than me,
abrupt & generous. We drank a glass of grog
to Independence.
              Returned, desiring the comfort
of family & friends, I am still Dull
remembering the Indians I saw in Alabama,
two thousand Cree in chains.
My trip to the Rockies is delayed.

A stranger on a London street once
gave me a paper bag with two live
Passenger pigeons in it to free
in English woods and return the favor
of colonization. The King joined
my list that day, of course he never paid
a Penny royal, and the species didn't settle England.

At Mill Grove, at twenty, I thought
I didn't know how to grow older,

nor thee, Lucy. Now
our two sons have taken wives,
welcome daughters.

When I earned a living by dancing
I had to push the shuffling students
like balky subscribers, singing
to assist them—finally, desperate,
dancing out the steps
& they applauded much, called for me
to dance & play at once
& I did, long hair tossed back
from the fiddle, I danced
at Bayou Sara, in Louisiana—
Lucy my wren, my cabbage, I'll do it again,
minuet us, trick us, mint us new.

VI. 1840–1851

Losses

It is the way of time itself
that starts in leisure
& rushes to a close. I spent two plates each
on 20 species when I began this Work, now I make composites
& even so am threatened by subscribers, & more than threatened,
who cancel because I exceed the 80 numbers promised.
They will not distract my Science when poverty has failed
that called me often to put down pencil & brush,
nor will I be ignored when I have finished the Birds,
though I am old. Today I write
a Prospectus for the Quadrupeds of North America,
though Bachman thinks me hasty. Hang
caution. Without work I fill with the deaths

of my dear daughters, my sons' wives.
They failed slowly, of consumption,
and now, four months apart, they are gone.
I want the coastal animals, the Beasts of central states,
the broad footed caribou, the badger, the omnivorous Bear,
boggy Moose among resinous hemlocks,
the desperate cats & other creatures of the Rockies, Mountains
of the Wind, I want them all: big as buffalos & elk, small
as shrews, fierce as Martens, I want bat, weasel, Bay-lynx,
I want all the varieties of squirrels
& the silver fox, the rat & red-tailed deer.
There is a space I must fill
until I can remember those two friends again
in place of the hurt they did me, dying.
Beloved Rosy, loved Eliza, it is a good time
to make a book, to build a house
where you will never live with us.

Letter to John Bachman

I built it, with my sons, a secluded house
of many rooms, riverfronted, bluff-backed
haven, verandahs all around
for conversations in which some remarks will be
the splash of seines & creak
of oars in oarlocks. Lucy & I will make our sleep
among the Hudson nightsounds
& smell its mud & moisture in our weather.
In a few weeks I'll plant a garden for her
and with Victor build a barn where I will draw.
Thirty acres will keep all we want
of livestock, fowls & pets & wild creatures.

Others travel now, Johnny gone for Californian gold
& Havell Jr come to America, his work with me over,
violently. He shipped 300 copper plates, his work
of a dozen years, & mine, to a warehouse in New York
that burned. I watched it,
pacing & furious (I suppose to the entertainment
of neighbors) & stalked home, smelling of smoke for weeks
& hair full of ashes.

I have been mistaken for a Quaker
because of my speech & habits of Industry
and now a long white beard
adds to the impression—Dunker, then.
Carpenter, farmer,
hunter. And scientist, man
who has made a home on the earth. Husband.

Sight

I am a collection of landscapes,
a Gazetteer. Of griefs & hopes
& consummations. I must be old now, although
I think so only in the company of mirrors. I cannot
summarize my self. Alone,
at American Falls, years ago,
I saw they were motion more
than Substance, wrote *cannot be drawn*
& walked behind into white
translucence, all hearing overwhelmed
& a moment's pull
to join broken things—my mill
engine failed, steamboat stolen,
Lucy's eight thousands dower lost
in Indigo embargoed, my self jailed—
outside saw a Traveller fold his cloak
neatly and fall
half in water, half in air

Wandered & drew Quadrupeds
& birds my passion
& as they do not pay
took faces of strangers in chalk, painted
street signs & a small weasel
to be graved for bank notes. Collected
for my America its wildness, made
distant grass & near Grebe
to shine alike with detail, clear
as water &

find my old mind composed
of what I saw

& cannot be seen again,
wilderness
moves away from us steadily

so Lucy & I drifted
by canopied Ark on darkened water
among slight mists
& bells of cows ashore, callings
of a Great Owl &
boatmen's horns at the next winding
while we floated to our first home

Old
light flows
above my last river
Hudson, I see the line
a goshawk leaves on the far shore's sky
ragged then smooth he rows through damp air
& glides. Chalk
wavers, lost, hands
vague *Can not see my line*
this third morning of Affliction

More steps than all the pennys lost & earned connect
our warm autumn honey-moon Ohio River,
Niagara its quartzy light & crash,
trains of blackbird & Pigeon
overhead, All motion & the same,
I fold my Easel

Reprise

I know them, their shapes & movements, their differing attitudes
of being still. I dream of balancing on the air
& when I wake it is to their noise, musings
that lift to raucousness. I have followed them
where no other man has gone, have shot
& ate them, or pierced & posed them on wires for Drawing,
have named & made them famous. I know
that a cormorant flies over water only, illustrating in the sky
the sinuous routes of rivers, I know pelicans fly low
until approaching land, at which they rise above gun range.
I know Herons contained will bite each other
to death. I have given a young dove
corn mush from my mouth else it would not eat.
Have cooked up a fish I found in the belly of a Pelican,
fresh swallowed, though Lehman gagged
& would have none. Have found the gannet provides
black & unpleasant meat. Have used the Grease of ducks
to keep my lips from cracking in the cold. I know them
and they me, at least some ways, so that a Gull hovers
to watch me eat but retires if I am crossed
with the burden of a long gun.
I have Acquired them without a shot,
have filled the calixes of flowers with sweet wine
so that the hummingbird falls, intoxicated.
I woke once to find a bittern on my bedpost
& wanting not to rouse the lodgers or damage the Inn
I whacked him with a broom.
I know Anhingas by the wheeze they make in sleep.
I rate the Mockingbird first for song, her rivals
the tawny & hermit thrushes, Catbird, Blue grosbeak.
The churr & chuck of blackbirds is my work song.
Stiff pointed wings of hawks produce

a whistling sound, & blunt Ducks wings whir.
I have heard my shot strike the Frigate bird in flight
& then the slapping of its wings in the disorder
of mortal fall. Others I have saved
& gave live to friends with several results,
a red egret that ate kitchen scraps & was gentle in the parlor
and the cranes Bachman killed & stuffed
because they first ripped ducks apart, then speared a cat
to the sunny ground on which it slept, & last began to stalk
his youngest child.

I once saw Gallinules in Regents park,
in London. Nearby some men with Ladies fed swans
& fat tame ducks, all of them making a fuss.
So be it. I regret
these labors only for thy absence. Why must I choose?
No, I do not. You attend me. I know
the Lady of the Waters, the Louisiana heron
with step so light it leaves no impression in the sand.
I am with others—I do not turn from company—
but when I am alone thy pressure on my mind appears,
thy look, though none sees,
& I travel lightly, by thee enabled.

Reprise

Where's the lamp? Wind
whines against the pane.
Plato? Zephyr? Dash?

No, I tell you. I will not wear spectacles.

Some big weather
builds. Do you hear
the waves?
           At sea. We need
music, but no screeching
cheap silk strings. Gut only
tames the watery stir.

Want my dogs. Can't stay.
Zephyr! Plato! Billy,
you go that way around the pond
& I'll go this way
& we'll get the ducks. Dinner

& songs & then to sleep
among the ferns.
Oh, good tobacco
& wool blankets
& stars!

Sur le pont de Nantes
a bridge gives a good view Billy
il y a t'un coq qui chante
but remember birds can see us too *la la*

Bon soir, madame,
bon soir. Who are you?

Notes

The information upon which this book is based comes from the works listed in the bibliography, especially from Herrick and from Audubon's journals. While I worked from historical accounts, I did not primarily intend to write history. Many of the incidents and thoughts in the poems are fictional; others are inventions around a bare fact; and some of the poems are assembled from material I read and recast in my own language. Occasionally I have quoted or paraphrased Audubon or his biographers, as detailed below. My goal was that my language take on the color of Audubon's so that the reader would find the poems seamless.

QUOTED

from Adams: lines 4–5, 8–11 of "Losses" (1)
from Audubon, *Ornith. Bio*: my subtitle; l. 27 of "At Coueron"
from Deloup: l. 15 of "At Ease"
from Ford, *Audubon by Himself*: "Billy . . . ducks" in "Reprise" (2), reported as Audubon's last words
from Ford, *1826*: much of "Spirits," except ll. 9–14 ("No, I will not . . . of my mother"; "No one . . . companion" and "My style puzzles" from "Letter to Lucy" (3); ll. 2–10 of "From My Journal"; ll. 10 and 13 of "Etude"
from Herrick, v. 1: epigraph; l. 20 of "Disaster"; "Joseph . . . parting" of "Losses" (1)
from Herrick, v. 2: ll. 11–12 of "Inventory. Journal."
from Proby: "Beneath . . . repellent" in "Wreck"

ADAPTED OR PARAPHRASED

from Adams: last line of "At Ease"; ll. 16–19 of "Letter to Lucy" (2)
from Audubon, *Ornith. Bio*: ll. 7–9 of "Losses" (2)
from Maria Audubon: ll. 13–15 of "Portraits"; stanzas 2, 3, 5 of "Inventory. Journal."
from Corning: ll. 30–34 from "Letter to Victor"; "electric . . . vigilant" of "I Am Restless"
from Ford, *Audubon by Himself*: "Risen . . . world" in l. 1 of "A Profitable Life"
from Ford, *1826*: ll. 17–23 of "From My Journal"; "I feel . . . walk" of "Interlude"

from Herrick, v. I: ll. I, 10–21, 26 of "Journal, at Sea"; ll. 12–13 of "Letter to Victor"
from Proby, passim: in ll. 8–42 "Reprise" (1).
"Edinburgh" was adapted from three sources: Adams; Ford, *1826*; Herrick, v. I.

Bibliography

Alexander B. Adams, *John James Audubon*. New York: G. P. Putnam's Sons, 1966.

John James Audubon, *Ornithological Biography. New.* New York: Abbeville Press, 1985.

Maria R. Audubon, *Audubon and his Journals*. New York: Dover Publications, 1986. (Unabridged republication of Dover edition of 1960; first edition, Charles Scribner's Sons, 1897).

Howard Corning, ed., *Letters of John James Audubon, 1826–1840*. New York: Kraus Reprint Co., 1969.

René Deloup, ed., *Vieilles Chansons et Rondes Françaises*. Paris: Editions Max Eschig, 1939.

Alice Ford, ed., *Audubon, by Himself.* Garden City, NY: Natural History Press, 1969.

————, *The 1826 Journal of John James Audubon*. Norman: University of Oklahoma Press, 1967.

Francis Hobart Herrick, *Audubon the Naturalist*, 2 vols. New York: Dover Publications, 1968.

Kathryn Hall Proby, *Audubon in Florida*. Coral Gables, FL: University of Miami Press, 1968.

Twelve Popular Old Rounds of France Brought Out Anew for the Enjoyment of Children and the Delight of Simple Souls. Boston: Boston Music Company, 1917.

UNIVERSITY PRESS OF NEW ENGLAND publishes books under its own imprint and is the publisher for Brandeis University Press, Brown University Press, Clark University Press, University of Connecticut, Dartmouth College, Middlebury College Press, University of New Hampshire, University of Rhode Island, Tufts University, University of Vermont, and Wesleyan University Press.

ABOUT THE AUTHOR

Pamela Alexander won the Yale Younger Poet award in 1984 for *Navigable Waterways* (1985) and has published poems in the *New Yorker* and *Atlantic*. After writing short persona poems on Amelia Earhardt and Howard Hughes, she says, "I had an urge to write longer poems about unusual people." Her interest in Audubon dates in part from childhood, when her mother, a veteran birder, "talked to me about ecology decades before the word was commonly used." She currently teaches in the Writing Program at the Massachusetts Institute of Technology

Library of Congress Cataloging-in-Publication Data

Alexander, Pamela, 1948–
    Commonwealth of wings : an ornithological biography based on the life of John James Audubon/Pamela Alexander.
    p.   cm.
ISBN 0–8195–2191–4. — ISBN 0–8195–1193–5 (pbk.)
    1. Audubon, John James, 1785-1851.   2. Ornithologists—United States—Biography.   3. Animal painters—United States—Biography.
I. Title.
QL31.A9A66   1991
598'.092—dc20

90–50908
[B]   CIP